THE
MAGIC COLOURS

Written by CECILIA EGAN

Illustrated by ELIZABETH ALGER

JB
BOOKS

ISBN 1 876622 06 7
This edition published in 1999.
Reprinted in 2001 by
J.B. Books Pty. Ltd.
P. O. Box 118
MARLESTON 5033
South Australia

First published in 1996 by Pan Macmillan Australia Pty. Ltd.

Publication copyright: J.B. Books Pty. Ltd
Story copyright: Cecilia Egan
Printed in Hong Kong through Phoenix Offset

National Library of Australia
Cataloguing-in-publication data available:
398.20994

FOREWORD

These wonderful legends of the native Australians have been adapted to be read and understood by children. Young ones too, can gain an insight into the rich and complex culture that existed for tens of thousands of years before Europeans landed.

The stories are not intended to be exact replicas of the original tales, but attempt to convey the narrative in a manner to which children can relate.

Titles in this series:

White Clay and the Giant Kangaroos
The Frog Who Wouldn't Laugh
The Willy-Willy and the Ant
Magic Colours

Long ago, so the Koori storytellers say, all birds were the same colour - black.   The rosellas and lorikeets, the galahs and cockatoos, the lyrebirds and wrens - all were black as burnt wood.

One evening a little black dove was flying around looking for food. He landed on a log to rest, but his foot was pricked by a sharp splinter.

The wound was so painful that he fell on his back calling for help. The other birds flocked around, anxious to assist him. Some brought beakfuls of water for him to drink...

...some washed the wound and tried to bandage it with leaves.

Only the crow did not help. In fact, he was cross because all this fluttering and chattering had disturbed his peace and quiet. He tried to frighten the other birds away!

The birds would not leave their friend the dove, who was becoming more ill by the minute. His foot was now swollen to three times its normal size, but the birds didn't know what they could do to fix it.

Suddenly a galah had an idea. There might be yucky stuff in the foot and if it came out the dove might get better. She flew down and pecked at the dove's swollen foot. The dove cried out in pain but then a strange thing happened!

A great fountain of beautiful colours came flowing out of the wound and splashed onto the birds. Pink, light grey and pure white splashed on the galah. She squawked with joy!

Red, green, purple, yellow, white and blue came spurting out and covered the other birds, who began to dance with delight. The lorikeets looked like rainbows! Only the crow missed out because he had not stayed close to the dove to help him.

The dove was feeling much better now - all the pain had gone. He was even happier when he found that he was now snow-white all over!

From that day, the birds have kept their lovely colours.